WHEN YOUR MARRIAGE NEEDS REPAIR

A no-nonsense tool
for restoring your marriage

Dr. David B. Hawkins, ACSW, Ph.D.

"Let each
of you regard
one another
as more
important
than himself."

—Philippians 2:3b (NASB)

Victor is an imprint of
Cook Communications Ministries, Colorado Springs, Colorado 80918
Cook Communications, Paris, Ontario
Kingsway Communications, Eastbourne, England

WHEN YOUR MARRIAGE NEEDS REPAIR

ISBN: 0-78143-472-6
First Printing, 2001
Printed in the United States of America

Editors: Greg Clouse, Craig Bubeck
Cover & Interior Design: Global Images and iDesignEtc.

ABOUT THE AUTHOR

A licensed clinical psychologist trained in the fields of social work and clinical psychology, Dr. David B. Hawkins, ACSW, Ph.D., has been in private practice for more than twenty years and specializes in domestic violence, adult and family issues, and marriage enrichment. Based in Longview, Washington, he is a certified domestic violence perpetrator treatment provider, certified forensic examiner, and a spiritual director. He also is a member of the National Association of Social Workers, Academy of Forensic Examiners, and the American Psychological Association. The author of several other books, including *See Dick and Jane Grow Up* (ISBN: 0-78143-498-X), David

cohosts a weekly radio program entitled "Experiencing Family," and was the host of an award-winning community television program called "Right Where You Live." He has been married to his wife, Diane (a nurse practitioner) for more than twenty-five years, and they have two grown sons. He enjoys snow and water skiing, hiking, kayaking, and running in recreational races in his free time.

"We come to love not by finding a perfect person, but by learning to see an imperfect person perfectly."

—*Anonymous*

INTRODUCTION

Perhaps the title of this booklet caught your attention because of problems in your marriage. You may be in a place in your marriage where you are experiencing growing pains. Perhaps your marriage has withered from the drying winds of neglect. Perhaps you have experienced a crisis that has awakened you to the need to pay closer attention to what is happening in your love life. You may be looking for something to return the joy to your marriage. You may be in a situation you feel is desperate. If something doesn't change soon, you may feel like you are going to make a radical decision. Whatever your circumstances, the aim of this booklet is to strengthen your marriage. There are ways to save your marriage from continuing on a downward spiral. Whatever your situation, I am glad that you are taking action. **Your Pocket Therapist** can help.

Obviously, this simplified primer is not meant to take the place of extensive marriage counseling or the reading of more exhaustive marriage manuals. Those books compete for the limited space on bookstore shelves and are certainly worthy of our attention. This booklet is meant to cover material found in those more lengthy books in a quick and practical manner.

This **Pocket Therapist** booklet has taken information from the best of the counseling books and addresses 90 percent of what is needed to repair most problems in marriages. For the remaining 10 percent, I would recommend the following:

- professional marriage counseling;
- reading most or all of the books recommended at the end of this booklet;
- both a and b.

Since the information in this booklet can repair up to 90 percent of marital problems, it may be just what you need. Take a look.

Marriages, and all intimate relationships for that matter, take a great deal of energy and fortitude to keep them working smoothly. I do not want you to be misled by the title of this booklet into thinking that a marriage can be repaired or maintained with ease. Nothing could be further from the truth. It takes work and focus. But if you focus on the goal of repairing your marriage and commit to using these basic principles, your marriage can be changed. Isn't that exciting? A little work goes a long way. Now on to the task at hand.

Nature of the Problem

Keeping the energy in a marriage has to be the most difficult task known to humankind. The statistics prove this fact. With the divorce rate hovering above fifty percent and remarriages faring little better, marriage appears to be a daunting task. Those who have experienced divorce swear off serious relationships forever, though their resolve rarely lasts. In spite of the discouraging odds, we were created for relationships, and our emotional compass seems to naturally point us in that direction. Besides, we have God's help in this matter, and He will not fail us. *(Phil. 4:13—I can do all things through Christ who strengthens me.")*

We are made for intimacy, and yet at times it all seems to be a cruel joke. If we are made for relating, why is it all so difficult? At times it seems a relationship is like a rock sander that chafes and irritates as "her" edges scratch against "his" rough spots. We experience unbelievable pressures every day that seek to erode our marital relationship. I suspect that you are reading **Your Pocket Therapist** to begin the search for answers to alleviate some of the excruciating pain that can result from an unsatisfying relationship. Seeking help is the first step toward solving problems, so you are already on your way.

"HE WHO DWELLS IN THE
SHELTER OF THE MOST HIGH

WILL REST IN THE SHADOW
OF THE ALMIGHTY.

I WILL SAY TO THE LORD, HE IS
MY REFUGE AND MY FORTRESS,

MY GOD, IN WHOM I TRUST."

— *Psalm 91:1-2*

I often tell my clients that a marriage is like an old, classic car. It needs lots of time and attention, and it is always getting older, needing constant tuning. If left alone out in the weather, it rusts and decays in no time. Of course, it then becomes useless and without value. Kept in good repair with consistent tuning, polishing, and attention, it will gain value with age. When well maintained, marriages increase in value. They cannot be ignored and be expected to run smoothly. It just will not happen. Most of us find this out the hard way. We notice when the decay has already taken its toll, and hard work must be done to bring it back to its original beauty.

Those who seek counseling are the small percentage who have noticed the decay and want to try to save things. While they often notice the trouble after much damage has been done, at least they are aware that something is wrong. I admire their courage to come to a total stranger and reveal the personal things in their lives. It takes a great deal of humility to admit that the marriage is at a critical stage. Yet I believe that those who attempt to repair a marriage, or work toward growth beyond mediocrity, are heroes. Using focused energy to restore a failing marriage is a valiant endeavor. It is easy to put on a front that all is well. You can line up the family, put on your best clothes, smile, pet the dog, and at just the right moment, click the camera. For an instant you can pretend that everything is fine. Wrong! Things are not fine and in fact will only get worse. Action is needed. Are you ready?

Problems must be faced. The work you put toward this goal may at first stir up troubled feelings brewing just below the surface. Initially your partner may not be ready to explore these feelings and take a look at your marriage. With concentrated work, however, troubled feelings can be replaced with positive feelings. Your marriage also affects your physical health. It has been shown that a satisfying relationship is closely related to your level of happiness and health. Therefore, the work is definitely worth your effort.

Initial attempts to repair longstanding problems in marriages are difficult. Marriage counseling is difficult. This is because by the time couples get to the therapist's office they have usually built up such huge reservoirs of animosity that it would take TNT to break them down. I trust you are picking up **Your Pocket Therapist** before things have reached that point. Even if things are in rough shape, you can effectively repair a marriage by applying effort in a few strategic places. We will be looking at those places. With the right attitude the work can be straightforward and a relief. It might not always be enjoyable, but it doesn't have to be as painful as repairing a root canal either!

Necessary Ingredients

One of the most important things I tell my clients is that they must bring three critical elements to our sessions. I say the same to you as you read this booklet. The first necessary ingredient is *goodwill*—the desire to make things better, including doing your part toward that end. You must be willing to lay aside your anger and any desire to retaliate. Revenge or the thought of it might feel good, but it destroys rather than builds a union. You must be willing to set that aside and try to look at things from your spouse's point of view. This is no easy task, however it can be much more rewarding than dwelling on how you have been wounded and the desire to get even.

Goodwill means that you *commit* yourself to really trying the principles in this booklet, even if you are skeptical about them working for you. You may be thinking things are too far gone or that these steps are simply too hard for you. Nonetheless, goodwill requires that you try the steps and give them a chance. The worst that can happen is that you end up feeling better about yourself for clearing away some of the emotional debris in your own life. What a risk!

The Scriptures also mandate that as much as we are able we are to strive to be at peace with others. *"Make every effort to keep the unity of the Spirit through the bond of peace"* (Eph. 4:3). We are to encourage one another even when we do not feel like it. It is quite amazing to watch couples treat one another with respect, and then see the positive feelings creep slowly back into the marriage. I call it "planting seeds and pulling weeds." We are restoring a garden to its original lushness.

I want to create a picture for you that I think might be helpful. It is a picture of a garden. The garden has paths running through it and places where the water naturally flows through the rocks, gurgling and bubbling in a grand display. But the garden has had a forbidding transformation. This garden, once lush, verdant, and bursting with the colors of spring, has now withered. The colors have faded into one sun-scorched, brown blur. The flowing water is gone, leaving cracked soil and chipping rock. As your eye scans the garden, you are struck by the lack of life. You can feel the discouragement and sadness that comes with death. The elements have tortured the garden, taking a very high toll. Where has the life gone?

This picture aptly describes what takes place in our marriages. The elements of neglect and abuse sap the life from our relational gardens. The color, indicative of health and life, has been drained. The water, symbolic of life-giving energy, has given way to dryness. But as with any garden, hope exists if there is energy for restoration. How can it be done? Using the analogy of the garden, we are *"planting seeds and pulling weeds."* Just like we would do with a garden, we intentionally set out to pull out the thorns and thistles that choke the life from the other plants. As we clear away the debris, we have some room to stir in fresh soil and plant new, healthy seeds. We purposely take the water of love and attention and apply it strategically to the nutritious soil. We are now ready for change.

With new seeds we encourage one another, even when we do not feel like it. Jesus Himself called us to be loving to those we don't love (toward our enemies; Luke 6:27). So much more must we act lovingly toward our spouses. Sometimes that means willfully attending to the garden, if only because we are committed to its restoration. We will talk more in the booklet about what the weeds and seeds look like, as well as about water for the soul; but for now it is enough to get the picture.

The second necessary ingredient that opens us up to positive change is *humility.* Of course this is closely related to goodwill. What exactly is humility? Humility (which interestingly stems from the root word *humus,* or soil) is giving away the need to be right. Humility means we don't take ourselves so seriously—

we're down to earth. It means having an accurate view of ourselves, not thinking of ourselves more highly than we should. It's sober judgment. Romans 12:3 says, "Do not think of yourself more highly than you ought, but rather think of yourself with sober judgment, in accordance with the measure of faith God has given you." This is hard to come by when it is so tempting to believe that we have already learned the answers to all of life's difficult questions. Personal and spiritual myopia causes us to elevate our position and dismiss the views of others.

The story is told of a corporate executive who is entertaining a visiting dignitary. During a board meeting, an assistant rushes into the meeting to interrupt, only to be told to remember Rule #6. This pattern repeats several times, and each time the executive calmly replies, "Remember Rule #6." Finally, the visiting friend can stand it no longer and asks what this Rule #6 is about. The executive smiles and replies simply, "Don't take yourself so seriously!" When the dignitary asks what the other rules are, the executive insists, "There are no other rules."

We would all do well to remember Rule #6. Think about it. Isn't it tempting to approach interpersonal difficulties with a sense of certainty about who is causing the problem? (And of course that person is not us!) Isn't it tempting to point a finger at others and put up all kinds of barriers to recognizing our part in the dilemmas of life? It is very challenging to admit our own fallibility. But to move toward change requires the self-discipline to question ourselves. We need to assume we do *not* have all the answers and *are* contributing to the problem. It remains to be determined where and how we are contributing.

Certainties

"If a man will begin with certainties,
he shall end with doubts; but if he will be
content with doubts, he shall end on certainties."

— *Francis Bacon*

The third necessary ingredient for change is *focus*. When I think about focus in my life, I think about being intentional about something I want to accomplish. That particular goal moves to the top of the list of my many activities. It becomes a priority. I have found that if I do not focus, and become intentional, my great plans will evaporate. Here today, gone tomorrow.

If instead you are intentional, deciding to focus on a goal, you will learn the potential obstacles and develop specific strategies to overcome them. Notice the key words in the previous sentence: *intentional, specific, strategies, focus*. Learn to apply those words to your life, and you will see change. The ability to focus energy on a particular problem enables us to find solutions. A great majority of your energy needs to be focused on those few areas needing attention. This booklet will help you with the focus part. The goodwill and humility are only going to happen as you are open to the work of God's Spirit in your life.

It is important to understand that you only have a limited amount of energy. If your marriage has reached the point where it needs repair, you are probably wasting a tremendous amount of energy holding grudges, backbiting, and tearing your spouse down. Instead of *cooperating* with one another, you have probably been *competing*. Instead of praying for your marriage and for your spouse, you have probably been rehearsing how you have been wronged. It has become a sadly enjoyable pastime. While this is very natural, it will not create a conduit for God to bring peace into your life. Resentment only creates a conduit for negative energy and the sapping of any goodness left in your marriage. Work on letting it go.

Many marriages crumble because they do not resolve problems. I'm sure that you can relate. These couples go around and around on the same issues. Fight after fight, nasty comment after nasty comment, interspersed with a few good times, and then back to the conflict. Then, as if surprised, couples say, "Things never change." How discouraging this can be when month after month, year after year, the erosion of the marriage makes the grass look so much greener beyond our fence. But as someone aptly reminded, "The grass may be greener, but it still has to be mowed."

Resolution

> "RESOLVE TO PERFORM
> WHAT YOU OUGHT.
> PERFORM WITHOUT FAIL
> WHAT YOU RESOLVE."
>
> —*Benjamin Franklin*

In considering what you have read, have you been able to find a reservoir of goodwill, humility, and the willingness to focus your energies on this situation? A lot is at stake. The demise of a marriage is no small event. A sour relationship can tax your life incredibly; a successful one can be tremendously fulfilling and satisfying.

What follows are six relatively simple techniques. If applied they will transform your marriage. They are all practical tools, useful in relationships besides marriage. Like the commercial says, "You can take care of the problem now, or wait until it gets worse and then go in for the major repairs." Can you muster both the goodwill and focus? Will you practice to develop some proficiency at them? I hope you are willing to make the investment. Would you say a simple prayer with me as we begin?

"Lord, you know my heart. You know exactly what I need to restore my marriage to what you designed it to be. I acknowledge Your promise that if I submit my life to You, You will take care of all my needs. So I submit my heart's desires to you, and I trust You to make all things in my life work together for my own good. Amen."

"WHEN WE ARE MAGNANIMOUS, LIBERAL IN OUR GIVING AS WELL AS SHARING OF OUR SELF, WE SHOW NOBLE CHARACTER AND AN ABUNDANCE OF SPIRIT AND STRENGTH."

—Alexandra Stoddard

Six Basic Strategies for Transforming Your Marriage

COMMUNICATION: First you must agree, no matter what, that you will regularly communicate with one another. Yes, you knew that I would mention that one, didn't you? It's so basic, and it's what we all expect to hear at the latest, greatest marriage seminar. In point of fact, it is so true that it cannot be left out.

In the initial stages of a relationship this is easy. So much to learn about each other, and so little time. There is interest, excitement, and maybe even a hormone or two thrown in. The attraction to each other is intense. But as time goes by, communication gets more difficult. The routine settles in as we make our way through finding a job, raising a family, and handling all the issues of life. Busyness, children, and obligations get in the way. Make the commitment right now that you will work hard to keep those lines of communication open to one another. Most importantly, commit to talk even when you are in a mood where you want to back away into silence. We all know silence and withdrawal can be the ultimate weapons in a marriage!

Take care that all of your communication is not about the dishes, feeding the dog, and paying the bills. This kind of talk does not bring closeness. One tool my wife and I use is called an endearment journal. At least that's what we call it. We have a journal by our bed and take turns writing notes to one another, often things that are sentimental and difficult to say. These notes are fun to read and leave a positive afterglow.

To improve communication you must agree that things need to be improved right now. If left unchecked, the marriage will continue to deteriorate. Believing that no problem exists or that things will heal themselves is denial. Marriages need regular attention. Any relationship left alone will surely die. Practice checking in with each other and ask how your spouse is feeling about the relationship. A regular evening out, dedicated to learning how you both are doing, works wonders. Remember that the best gifts you can give your children are happy parents.

Communication is especially important when you do not feel like communicating. Anger is a primary culprit in creating roadblocks to communication. Anger narrows our vision. We are prone to blame, amplify, and generally distort things. Guard your emotions, especially anger.

Communication may also be blocked when your feelings have been hurt or when you are preoccupied with something that you believe may be more important at the time. Communication is like money in the bank when it comes to saving your marriage. There are several techniques that I would like to teach you that fall under the heading of communication. Each one is important for keeping the lines of communication open.

1. *ACTIVE LISTENING:* Give your spouse your undivided attention. Face each other and look into each other's eyes. Make comments that let the other person know you are with him or her emotionally. Nodding your head, and perhaps a gentle touch, will show your spouse that you hear what is being said.

2. *ACTIVE EMPATHY:* With active empathy you repeat what your spouse says in different words to convey that you are with him or her emotionally. You reflect back what you hear being said. Put yourself in your spouse's shoes and imagine what it is like to be in his or her place (for instance, married to you).

3. *PERCEPTION CHECKING:* To check your perception, you summarize what you are hearing and ask if what you heard is accurate. It may surprise you to hear how often what you thought you heard is *not* what he or she is trying to convey.

4. *ASKING QUESTIONS:* While counterproductive if overused, questions show your spouse that what he or she says is interesting. People enjoy and benefit from sharing their stories. You can assist your spouse by asking questions that encourage further self revelation. Open-ended questions that do not call for a yes or no answer can be very helpful to a discussion. Your spouse will be pleased that you want to know more about him or her.

5. *ASKING FOR CLARIFICATION:* When listening to your spouse, ask for clarification to make sure you really understand. You may want to explain what you think you're hearing, but wonder if that is what he or she is really saying. Usually your efforts to accurately hear will be greatly appreciated.

6. *VALIDATING YOUR SPOUSE'S PERCEPTION AND RIGHT TO HAVE IT:* This may seem like a simple task, but it may be harder than you think. Many of us hold to our points of view with such an ironclad grips that we tend to get fixed and rigid. We see our point of view as irrefutable. Of course, the tighter we hold on to our point of view, the greater the conflict. During your next

disagreement with your spouse, work hard at accepting his or her opinion, regardless of whether you agree with it.

Practicing these simple communication tools assists you in transforming the way you talk to your spouse. You will notice a warming in the emotional climate.

MORE ON LISTENING. Second, and closely related to the first tool, is learning to really listen to your spouse. Listening is a skill that can be developed. We all need to be heard and, more importantly, understood. There is a part of our innermost selves that needs attention and recognition. If this need is left unmet, we may seek it from other sources: other people, our jobs, our hobbies. Take the time to really get to know your spouse. What are his or her likes and dislikes? What are his or her emotional and physical needs? Moreover, do you know what your spouse needs from you? Someone has said that love means being willing to meet the other's deepest needs. Take time to find out just what those needs are.

Take a moment right now, if you dare, and ask your spouse what it would take to improve your relationship. Be prepared for some honest feedback. If you listen to the feedback and act upon it, your marriage will undoubtedly improve.

There is something I call *soulful listening* that enhances a relationship as well. This involves listening for the themes and deep passions that exist in your spouse far below the surface. We are each created with unique gifts and longings. Do you know what they are in your spouse? He or she may never talk about them, at least not in so many words. To truly understand someone, you have to tune in, day after day, week after week. You may have to ask questions and explain what you are hearing, because you will likely hear your spouse's "soul" more clearly than he or she does. If you can help your spouse articulate this soulfulness, intimacy is sure to follow. As the saying goes, intimacy means *"into me see."*

DEVELOPING SHARED INTERESTS: Third, you must agree to keep interests growing between you. At the start of the marriage, this was not hard. You loved being with one another and enjoyed every moment. At that time anything you did together was likely to be enjoyable. It did not take much effort or creativity. As time goes on, distractions become greater, and it gets harder to stay excited together. It can be done, however, if you will agree to pursue mutual interests and activities that are enjoyable to each of you. Believe it or not, all of the possibilities for interest and excitement in each other still exist and can be fostered. Think about it.

Sadly, many of the people who seek counseling or separate have lost the passion for their spouses. They have forgotten what attracted them to their spouses in the beginning. It can be a fun exercise to reminisce and remember the attraction of the early days. Perhaps you can "Rejoice in the [spouse] of your youth" (Proverbs 5:18). It's all still there; it may just be buried. Again, where is your focus? How much time and energy will you commit to recreating your relationship so that you will again enjoy one another's company?

Yes, I know that many activities will clamor for your attention. Most of them are worthwhile and good for you and others.

They may be very gratifying, but before you know it, it has been months since you have been out for a romantic dinner with your spouse. All of these other activities will gradually eat up the time and energy that you used to devote to one another. You can unconsciously come to believe that the marriage can care for itself. Wrong! Your marriage is more important than any of those other activities. Don't wait until something breaks down before you do your routine maintenance.

Right now sit down and list several things that you both enjoy but haven't taken the time to do for awhile. If the relationship has begun to stagnate, it may take some exploration to find the things that were once enjoyable and can be again. Brainstorm about the things that you would like to do together in the future. Develop an agreement to take the time in the future to weave these activities into your life. Better yet, make an agreement that you will create time for yourselves on a consistent basis: once a week or two times a month. Then hold each other accountable to stick to the agreement. Begin again to reach out and create a little adventure. You will find that romantic youthfulness within is still alive and well and even longing for a little excitement.

You may be saying to yourself at this point that there are no areas of mutual interest. That is almost never true. Lack of mutual interests makes the task larger, but not insurmountable. Embark upon the adventure of creating and finding new areas interesting to both of you. Agree to start with each person participating in an activity that excites the other. Again the keys are *goodwill*, *humility*, and *focus*. It *can* be done.

KEEPING THE ROMANCE ALIVE: Fourth, you must work diligently to keep the romance alive in your marriage. If you don't, there may be others outside the marriage who *will* spend the effort on your spouse. No one wants that to happen. There is no deeper pain or tragedy in a marriage than the couple who struggles with betrayal. Fortunately, it can be avoided. Again, persist at doing the little things that keep the romantic fires aflame. It is not, as many imagine, huge actions that create the romance, but rather the attitude that exists on a day-in, day-out basis.

" AWAKE, NORTH WIND, AND COME,
SOUTH WIND. BLOW ON MY GARDEN,
THAT ITS FRAGRANCE MAY SPREAD ABROAD.
LET MY LOVER COME INTO HIS GARDEN
AND TASTE ITS CHOICE FRUITS. "

—*Song of Songs 4:16*

For example, do you make gracious comments to one another when leaving or greeting at the end of the day? Do you make a special effort to touch and treat your spouse with kindness when you are together? These simple niceties go a long way toward creating a loving, romantic environment. Again, take care not to let the concerns of the day choke out the tenderness. Perhaps you can agree to try the endearment journal. A scripture that would be good to memorize is the following: *"Do not let any unwholesome talk come out of your mouths, but only what is helpful for building others up according to their needs, that it may benefit those who listen"* (Eph. 4:29).

Take a few moments to remember the things that meant so much at the start of the marriage. What special things did you do together that created such romance? Can you revive the enthusiasm to try them again? You may be feeling awkward about adding this dimension to your life again. After all, you've been together for so many years now, why do you need romance? You don't really believe that, now do you? We are never too old to long for that special feeling, and you can have it again, with effort and focus.

"In a dark time,
the eye begins to see."

—*Theodore Roethke*

Focus

Some of you may be saying that it is too late. You picked up this booklet really thinking that the problem has gone on too long. You may be saying to yourself, "I don't feel anything for him/her anymore." This certainly has to feel discouraging, and perhaps frightening. Yet there still is hope. I have seen many marriages renew the spark after years of fading embers. *Believe that it isn't too late.* Make one special effort, followed by one more, and soon a spark is glowing.

If you are one of those people who is reading this with more skepticism than hope, let me offer you a challenge. For twelve weeks make renewing your relationship with your spouse your number-one priority. Put other activities aside, whatever they may be. Get into some good counseling. Practice pulling weeds and planting seeds. Pulling weeds means that, **one by one**, you will look at the issues that are causing resentment. While you are looking at the issues, you will also be planting the seeds of kindness. Practice the skills in this booklet. See what happens. You may be very surprised. Make the commitment.

One more comment on the little things. Let's not make the job too overwhelming. I am talking about a pleasant comment here, a compliment there, a light non-sexual touch here, a bit of help-fulness there. These little things will be the foundation upon which the love will be rebuilt. Take the time to buy special gifts, send flowers, go out on dates. Dress up for each other. Keep your appearance attractive even behind the closed doors of home. It matters. These *little* acts will pay great rewards. These *little* efforts, done once in a while, have a *huge* effect. These niceties go a long way toward dissipating the tensions that build up from the daily struggles that occur in your marriage.

A simple kindness melts a lot of resentment.

It may be tempting to think that romance is an option in marriage. Many other areas demand our time and attention, and romance usually takes a back seat to more pressing concerns. When our focus is on work, bills, housekeeping, and the children, is it any wonder that our romantic desires for our spouse begin to dim? Keep in mind that both spouses must keep romance a priority in the marriage to keep the spark alive. However, if *one* will begin, the other has the opportunity to follow.

CONFLICT RESOLUTION SKILLS: Fifth, you must develop an effective way to resolve your differences. If you have no method for resolving problems, your marriage cannot weather the storms that are bound to come your way. All marriages have problems: finances, children, sexual difficulties, or living in a blended family. Some concerns center around a spouse struggling with alcohol or drug addiction. However, the obvious problem is often not the real problem. Can you talk about these problems and find solutions? Can you find a way to resolve those endless, petty conflicts? Let's review several key concepts when it comes to fighting fair and resolving conflicts.

1. *KEEP THINGS IN PERSPECTIVE:* When we get angry we usually distort the problem, making it worse than it really is. Try to step back from the issue and ask yourself, "Is this issue as big as I am making it?" Be careful not to blow things out of proportion.

2. *KEEP YOUR EMOTIONS UNDER CONTROL:* Too often hurtful things are said when we feel emotionally overwhelmed. I believe it is important for either spouse to be able to call a time-out if things

> **"LIFE IS NOT A PROBLEM**
> **TO BE SOLVED,**
> **BUT A MYSTERY TO BE LIVED."**
>
> —*Thomas Merton*

get too tense. The other spouse must respect this time-out and agree to set the issue temporarily aside. Then, the spouse originally calling for the time-out must set a time when both will gather again to work on the issue. If the issue remains too hot to handle, I recommend a third party, preferably a trained therapist, who will help navigate these rough waters.

3. *NEVER HIT BELOW THE BELT:* Be careful about saying things that you will regret later. There is never a place for name-calling, intimidation, or threatening your spouse. This is a quick way to erode the respect your spouse has for you. Guard against bringing up painful intimacies previously shared; you run the risk of ending all trust in the future.

4. *ACCEPT YOUR PART OF THE PROBLEM:* Admit it when you have been wrong. This includes not blaming your spouse, realizing that blame only raises defenses and escalates the fighting. It does nothing to defuse the conflict. Say you are sorry and wrong when the shoe fits. It does wonders to keep an attitude of humility in your marriage.

5. *PRACTICE THE FOLLOWING COMMUNICATION SKILLS:*

    a) Really listen to, and understand, the other's point of view;

    b) Reflect that you understand your spouse's point of view;

    c) Give your spouse the right to that point of view, even if it differs from your own;

    d) Share your point of view, at a time you will be listened to;

    e) In a nondefensive manner, discuss how you see things differently;

    f) Talk in "I" language about your point of view. Avoid talking about "you";

    g) Agree upon a compromise/solution suitable to you both.

I have just mentioned several critical issues that must be followed if you are to work through conflict in a healthy way. Too many couples find themselves in a win/lose battle. Each try to *force* the other to see things his or her way, even using shame tactics in the hopes that the other will "see the light." If you haven't noticed, this is a total waste of time and shows a lack of respect for the other person. There are many equally valid points of view. Most couples make the mistake of failing to abandon their arguments and creatively look for ways they can agree and move forward with the solutions. As a way of making the necessary shift in thinking, consider saying these words: "Now that we agree that we see this differently, what are some ways to work through this problem?" Effective work in this area of respecting your spouse's differing points of view can literally save your marriage.

Another very real problem that happens in the way that couples communicate is what I call "*trauma patterning*." In other words, couples get used to talking to one another in exactly the same ways, each and every day. Unfortunately, the way that they communicate involves many very destructive and traumatic patterns. They include belittling the other's point of view, name-calling, ignoring the other, blaming and accusing the

Growth

"GROWTH OCCURS IN SPURTS.
YOU WILL LIE DORMANT SOMETIMES.
DO NOT BE DISCOURAGED.
THINK OF IT AS RESTING."

—*Julia Cameron*

other of being the sole cause for their problems. It often includes attacking known areas of vulnerability. If you choose to attack your spouse in these ways, or other ways that you know are destructive, you will be living in a constant state of trauma and self-defense. Growth cannot occur. Agree to discuss how you resolve problems and to eliminate the possible trauma patterns that you repeat with each other.

Much of the trauma we experience, and inflict upon one another, comes from blaming and shaming our spouses. The Scriptures are clear about the proper attitude and behavior we are to have toward each other. *"You, therefore, have no excuse, you who pass judgment on someone else, for at whatever point you judge the other, you are condemning yourself, because you who pass judgment do the same things"* (Rom. 2:1).

THE IMPORTANCE OF COMMITMENT: The sixth and final step toward having a fulfilling marriage is the agreement that you are *committed* to making this marriage work. In a time when the word *commitment* does not come up very often, we would all do well to reconsider our commitments. When it comes to marriages, we have too often treated them as a dispensable commodity. How many of us are guilty of thinking, "If it doesn't work out I'll just move on"? Unfortunately, many in our society have done just that. By committing to your marriage, you no longer contribute to this disposable mentality.

At the beginning of **Your Pocket Therapist** I stated that the three primary things that you needed to bring to this work were *goodwill, humility,* and *focus.* Part of the issue of focus has to do with commitment. You can never accomplish anything without

> ## "HE IS POOR INDEED THAT CAN PROMISE NOTHING."
>
> —*Thomas Fuller*

Commitment

focus and subsequently, commitment. So I am suggesting that you decide, right now, to make the commitment to make this marriage work. If all else fails, commit at least to the twelve-week "seed planting" exercise.

Perhaps the biggest robber of our commitment is the false notion that things will always be better somewhere else. Be careful to not daydream and fantasize about getting out of the marriage. The problem is not "out there," but rather "in here."

We all know that the grass looks greener on the other side of the fence. However, every bit of energy we put into thinking about the greener grass is energy that we are not using to work on our marriage and our personal issues. Our spouse can usually sense that we are not really available for the relationship, and this can create tremendous distrust and a lack of safety. For certain people this is bound to reawaken very fragile issues. When they sense that you are not really committed, they pull out emotionally as well. Thus, you have effectively created a self-fulfilling prophecy. When we tell ourselves, "This is never going to work," we are probably predicting the future of our marriage. The Lord makes us an amazing promise. *"Delight in the LORD, and he will give you the desires of your heart" (Psalm 37:4).*

Therefore, consider telling your spouse that you are in this marriage for the long haul. This can be a beautiful way to create trust and safety so that further growth is possible. An extra benefit is that you too find yourself giving more value to the marriage, even if you are struggling with your own level of commitment. Every ounce of energy you invest increases the chance of success and happiness.

Trust

"TAKE SHORT VIEWS,
HOPE FOR THE BEST,
AND TRUST IN GOD."

—*Tobias George Smollett*

A FINAL THOUGHT

God has made available to you tremendous power with which you can, in effect, create a new environment. You have been endowed with tremendous creative talents and abilities. You can use those abilities in either constructive or destructive ways. In the interest of self-preservation, some of us have spent a lot of time developing self-destructive patterns. These are intricate patterns, which we repeat day in and day out. They perpetuate negativity in our lives. We usually are not aware of these repeated behaviors and attitudes that stunt our growth and inhibit our success. Relationships happen to be one primary area where we replay these sad, silly, self-defeating patterns. Are you ready to move forward and believe that you have something marvelous to give to your marriage—and to receive from your marriage?

Of course, making a marriage healthy is not easy; it is one of the most difficult things you will ever do. It is also one of the most rewarding. There is nothing quite like the feeling of practicing these steps, planting seeds, and seeing your marriage blossom. If your marriage blossoms, you will blossom as well. I must also add that the lessons we experience in our marriage are designed for our growth. It's like going to school—you can skip class, but you have to learn the lesson later on. That is, we tend to repeat the mistakes that we make in each of our relationships. If we do not learn it the first time, the lesson will surely come back around another time. You can get away from your spouse, but you can't get away from you.

So build up your courage, drop your resentment and your guard. Eat a little crow if necessary and get down to the task of rebuilding this marriage. If you will start, your spouse is likely to follow at some point. Working on marriage problems is like a delicate dance—one step at a time, with lots of smiling, and cutting each other a lot of slack. Each step of progress deserves lots of encouragement. This is a new dance, and you need to lighten up. Don't forget to have a little fun along the way if you start to take yourself too seriously. Blessings to you as you strive to strengthen your marriage.

SHARE YOUR STORY

Throughout the development of this book series, we have been introduced to many exceptional individuals. We are interested in hearing your stories. We want to share your experiences so that we in turn can share them with others. Please send your thoughts to:

Your Pocket Therapist
Dr. David B. Hawkins
1801 First Avenue, Suite 3B
Longview, WA 98632
(360) 425-3854

Dr. Hawkins has established an exciting web site that offers encouragement for families. The site features help on family issues, links to other relevant sites, and information about setting up seminars or speaking engagements.

Visit his ministry at www.InCourageMinistry.com.